moving day

moving day

Terence Young

John Barton, Editor

Signature EDITIONS

Cover design by Terry Gallagher/Doowah Design.
Cover photo by Terence Young.
Photo of Terence Young by Patricia Young.

This book was printed on Ancient Forest Friendly paper.
Printed and bound in Canada by Marquis Book Printing Inc.

We acknowledge the support of The Canada Council for the Arts and the Manitoba Arts Council for our publishing program.

Acknowledgements
I would like to thank John Barton for his fine editorial advice and for his encouraging words during the preparation of this book. Thanks are also due to Patricia, who has always been my patient and wise teacher. I am grateful, too, to my children, Cléa and Liam, who have inspired many of these poems and to whom I dedicate this second volume.

Versions from this collection have appeared in the following journals: *Prairie Fire*, *Event*, *The Fiddlehead*, *Vintage*, *Grain*, *The Malahat Review*, and *Arc*.

Library and Archives Canada Cataloguing in Publication

Young, Terence, 1953–
Moving day / Terence Young.

Poems.
ISBN 1-897109-11-3

I. Title.

PS8597.O72M69 2006 C811'.54 C2006-904166-0

Signature Editions
P.O. Box 206, RPO Corydon, Winnipeg, Manitoba, R3M 3S7
www.signature-editions.com

for Cléa and Liam

Contents

When You Become Young Again

Hostages

Brave

When You Become Young Again

Saturday Wine Tour on the E&N

The city conforms, divides itself into triangles along the right-
of-way, which was here first. Beyond the window of the day

liner, the rough side of town appears and disappears, a fabric
of property values diminishing, through which we weave like

the shuttle of a loom while women dole out champagne, pass
canapés up and down the aisle. Since this is not a fantasy, the

bread is slightly stale. We hold out our glasses for seconds,
while the engine gathers steam for the steep climb ahead.

You elbow your way to the washroom, return with news of the
open track, how it peered up your skirt. When the ground

falls away beneath us like the trough of a giant green wave,
I look down to imagine the boy who jumped out of his life

in this same spot, and his friends who searched the pools and
caves along the river, believing they could find him. I wonder

how, after a day like that, there could ever be one like this,
a slender flute that will fill and empty and fill again with Valley

Mist, Ortega, Angelique. The last of my uncles travels with us,
a man so like my dead father I cannot resist the worn cliffsides

of his voice, the urge to let go and sail into the buoyant air of
memory. At each vineyard on the circuit, I raise a toast to the

past and listen to the pretty speeches of the oenologists.
Their facts fall at my feet like freshly pulled corks, but I am a

student out on a school field trip waiting for my free sample. On
the other side of twelve-foot fences, deer yearn to reach the soft

canopy of grape leaves. They wait like standing water, and their
eyes are deep as the night sky. Above our heads starlings send

scouts to find the ripest fruit for the flock. At the end of the day,
Gary, whose girlfriend is a teacher, sits on the grass by the railway

station. His dog is called Amadeus. Like Mozart, he contends.
He tells us when the Haida were around, no one was safe.

"Guess what," he says. "It's all true." On the trip home we face
the right way. You say there's something about a child waving

at a train, and for a moment I become the boy beneath
the clothesline, see our faces in the window as we roar by.

Wild Blackberries

Among the strands of sun-
burnt grass, there are enough
to fill a slim volume
of poetry.

You held a bowl of pancake
batter thirty years ago, the
summer our six big firs came
down and every low plant that
used to grovel in their shade went
wild in light that had not touched
the ground for centuries. I watched
the fruit you'd gathered disappear
with each turn of the
mixing spoon.

Upon the tongue
a prick of memory, one molecule
nudging another along nerve ends
that lead through giant ferns and
alder and honeysuckle to my father,
his khaki pants creased,
their cuffs full of cigarette ash,
bending down to pull aside bracken, fallen
branches, to pluck my first taste,
a berry that meant nothing more to me then
than what it carried of the forest earth,
the flies that gathered
in the lazy air.

Still Somewhere

Maples grow now
where the firs once stood,
those dangerous old fellows
who leaned over our house
like subway riders, curious to see
what we were reading.

I miss them,
the big guy most of all,
how he made us shimmy
twenty feet of rope
to the first branch, and from there
a stairway,
at least that's how the brave
described it.

They've been gone
for decades now,
each stump a ruin,
a cut healing back to earth,
their trunks no more than memory,
imaginary columns of air,
and the empty spaces in the canopy
still closing or closed.

Gone more than half my life,
yet, in tree time, nothing,
and, left alone,
they would have died
years before they finally fell.

Even now
it's easy to imagine
they're still somewhere,
while the speedy maples
stretch themselves thin,
hungry for the light, glad-handing
every breeze that passes,
unable to believe their luck.

Prelude to the Afternoon

The deer tucks her legs under, hides them,
not unlike a collapsible bridge table
collapsing. From a perch on the hill,
she looks about: moss, fir,
slim Garry oak.

Her big lids shut for seconds
at a time. Overhead a squirrel gathers
acorns as fast as children gather
quarters and dimes and fifty-cent pieces
in their dreams.

Inclining, the deer twists off
a stalk of grass, takes a bite and chews,
only the breeze, the busy squirrel and
a pair of stereophonic ravens
to pull her from her brown study.
Her mouth works fitfully, as though
the scene has provoked an idea,
prodded a memory, as though this
is a period for reflection,
an interlude:

a deer dealing with the day,
coping with these hours
that are everybody's hours.

A roofer pausing,
sound of the last nail fading.
A strawberry picker at the end
of one row, the next one not yet
in her mind.
A surfer between waves.

To think she is taking
a break here. That she is resting
the way others consider rest — a cessation,
something other. She chooses to sit,
to stand, to bend her head,
and choice suggests a will,
even if she wills no more
than this.

When You Become Young Again

You think it will be familiar,
that you will be barefoot,
the soles of your feet near burning
on a manhole cover
as you walk to the beach,
a last bite of Popsicle still clinging
to the stick.

Or that chimney smoke and snow will mix
in the bright air of a November night
next to a woodshed
where you are kissing a girl
whose touch,
even through the thick wool of her mittens,
carries the conviction of her choice.

You think you can predict the form
your journey will take,
how the past will appear to you,
a dream you will one day learn
to summon at will.

But instead you are here,
outside Bakersfield, California,
the power poles converging in front of you
along Route 99,
and the hills outside Los Angeles
rising like memories
from the hot air of a history
you have never known.

The Plum Trees

They spiral out of the ground,
a double helix.

Male and female, a friend says,
and I believe him.

Everything about them is excessive.

Fruit dangles in bunches every August.
Aphids weep goo on the lawn chairs,
wasps gorge on aphids and later
on the decomposing plums which are no good
for wine or jam.

Underground, they spread suckers
in all directions.
A filigree of roots chokes the drains.

Cut them down, my wife says.

But I start thinking: our son,
chinning the lower branches, our daughter
galloping like Belle Star around their twin trunks.
The idea smells of murder.

Roses wither, bulbs rot.
Grapes die on the vine. No matter
how much I water, the grass remains
tawny and thin. Even the buttercup
loses its grip.

My friend suggests poison
to control growth, radical pruning.
Separate them, he says. Give them something
to cry about.

In the end, the plum trees
squeeze out the sun
and drape the yard in darkness.

My wife tells me it's a matter of survival.

Now when the temperature drops,
I rummage through the woodpile for a piece:
heavier than oak, grain like blood,
it burns long and hot and bright.

Returning

Eastern lakes are drying up.
Waterfront cottages look out on acres of sand,
their wharves like boardwalks going
nowhere.

In the west,
mountain snowpacks are so deep
they crush the steel pylons
that hold up the province's electrical lines.
Valley dwellers wait for spring melt,
count the inches between their front steps and
the rising brown that slops
against the crumbling river bank.

Everywhere people are asking for the past.
They want the ancient names of their countries restored.
They want the sea to reveal its hidden wrecks,
to draw back its waves and return
the hundreds of men and women it swallowed
on a single night.
They want the stars to stop talking.

If only we could pass a law.
Maybe then the children would leave each other alone.
Maybe the fish would remember where they were born.
Maybe we could lie in the sun again.

In a bar, one man
talks to another. He spends his regrets like loose coins,
while on the darkening street outside
a boy on a skateboard makes good
his escape.
Inside the abandoned pack,
the policeman finds a novel the boy is studying for school,
the corner of one page folded down

to mark where the boy stopped reading,
where the policeman now begins.

The Benediction

It's June, near dusk. Across
the street two teams of little leaguers are
slugging it out with whoops and
insults:
Kill the pitcher, he's a belly itcher.
Tom and I are walking to the corner store
for licorice
when Gary Prescott blocks our path and
tells us to get down on our knees.
He is two grades ahead of us,
already shaving and hair like a rain cloud.
We are to tell him that our mothers
have sex with each other,
that our fathers lick our sisters like dogs.
I know nothing
about the past, about what is rare and
what is commonplace.
Everything, even cruelty, is
a mystery I am willing to learn.
I do not know my friend
will refuse to speak of this night
for as long as I know him,
or that more than the warm cement
against my skin
or the impossible couplings I am forced to utter,
I will remember the neighbour,
the one who witnessed it all
through the picture window of his living room.
I will remember how he put on his glasses
and leaned upon the sill
to see more clearly a couple of
nine-year-old boys,
hands behind their backs,
lips moving in unison as they bowed
before another boy, who laughed and
patted them on their heads,
an induction into something,
a blessing, perhaps,
though at that distance, it must have been
hard to say.

Drinking Games

The boy who holds a card
must not speak English.
        Hola, he tries. *Como está?*

Next to him,
a girl counts on her fingers,
clothes dripping from
a plunge in the pool.

Thirteen, she declares.
        Everybody holds hands.

What's a multiple? someone asks.
The room agrees:
        a fair question.

From a deck of forty-nine the same girl
takes a rule card:
        No articles, she says now.

Give me beer!

Memories are made of this. Dean Martin
in his drunken drawl,
        that stool, the cigarette.
Tonight it's warmer:
a Pacific breeze shakes the edge of the palapa,
geckos chirp from behind palm fronds
        and light fixtures.

I regret my youth,
even though Byron warned me not to.
        Why live? the poet said,
and he was dying.

No drinking games as I recall.
No slow, comic tightrope
        from sober to drunk.
Pound, my friends would say. A whole *twixer*
and we just pounded her.
        Her.

I remember the penalty box
at a local rink, the floor slippery
with vomit.
A band was playing.
        Playing.

I used to believe I could tell
the amateur from
        the professional,
the drinkers who were in it for
        the heartache it promised
from the weekend dilettante.

Do you find this disturbing or just
ridiculous? a boy asks.

His eyes are bloodshot, vacant,
almost reptilian.

You lose, the crowd says,
        and he nods,
tips the bottle back.

Spotter

Above your head
a boy straddles the high bar.
He is talking himself into something,
his latest trick, a name like a drink:
rigor mortis,
double with a twist.

You plant your feet, extend your arms,
anticipate distance, weight.
The instructor says you are here
to absorb impact, to crumple if necessary
like the fender of a car.

You think of your neighbour in his new
Fairlane, the acres of chrome
and the green wings that carry him
to work.

You think of the friends who stood by and
watched you trade twenty dollars
for five hits of windowpane,
how they cheered
when you swallowed three at once,
talking you through
the long night and day that followed.

There is no end
to the things we place between ourselves
and disaster.
The seat belts, the life jackets, the steel
guard that directs the carving knife away
from your father's wrist:
every moment you are alive
is an exercise in trust.

And when the boy's hands finally fail,
his body spinning toward you like a pilot
shot out of his doomed plane,
you lower him carefully onto the sea of blue
tumbling mats, words already forming
on your lips, a tip on technique,
whatever it takes to get him up,
try again.

Remembrance Day, 1996

The kitchen clock is a black-
jack dealer flipping eleven.
I take my coffee into
the backyard, wait
for the guns to fire.

Our garden is finally dead,
a cemetery of stalks and
blasted pods. Starlings crowd
the pointless grapevine.
(I tell myself again
the plum trees will have to go.)

Nobody notices me remove myself
from this holiday morning.
I slip away in a cloud
of purpose, the handyman's
prerogative: Are the drains
draining, is the fence dividing?

On the other side of the hedge,
the neighbour's daughter
has collected a few friends
to honour the fallen.
She hushes a boy who is giggling.

Eleventh hour, eleventh day,
eleventh month. The ritual of
memory where only the ritual
remains.

From the harbour now
a percussive blast signals — the start,
the finish?
A more suitable
New Year, it suddenly seems to me.
I imagine solemn young heads
bowing. Somebody asks,
Isn't there supposed
to be a trumpet?

Don't Look Back

I found a light bulb,
its filament still intact,
in the middle of a street
in Mexico.

It brought to mind a friend
who came upon two batteries
stuck in the mud.
He said he'd always
wondered what made the world
run.

I said nothing
when I found the light bulb,
though briefly,
while I was carrying it home,
I thought of Bob Dylan, and of course
my friend.

The batteries my friend found
were dead. They weren't a miracle the way
my light bulb was.
They merely served
as the basis for witty observation
made over thirty years ago.

A light bulb brings to mind
the delicate carapace of the brain,
how it is easily shattered.

As for the Mexican street,
its surface was corrugated cement,
unforgivingly hard, dotted with mangos,
fallen and split open. Traffic
wasn't heavy, but continuous.

On Waking from an Afternoon Nap

For now
        the feet upon the stairs
have no owner. The dog at odds
outside is just a dog.

And it will take time
        to name this room,
to place the day,
the season.

Weren't there some wars? A space
        program?

Gaps shrink,
the approaching tide fills
        the reasonable shore, now foul and muddy.

There is an apple I prefer — the Gravenstein,
and that pewter mug I bought a friend,
a "graven stein," too.

A marvel, really,
all these bits that come together like a
a math equation when it looms
into sense:
        I live here,
        these are the people I love.

Yes, I remember I used to spin and
spin myself about, eyes shut,
just to watch the whirling world
find its feet again.

Hostages

Woke Up This Morning, Looked Round for My Shoes

I was taking a walk. Perhaps it was a Saturday. I remember
closing the door behind me. I remember thinking I was gone.

The whole city was a Paris peep show. Squares of cement
passed beneath me like the pages of a girly magazine. *Psst.*

Hey, meester. The sky was a contract laid out on a banker's
desk. Sign here, it said. If I had a wife, then where was she?

And the streets so insistent, so loud with their dying trees.
They swallowed me up, if you want to know. They ate me

like Halloween candy. For a while I was walking with dogs,
but the dogs ignored me. I tossed sticks and reached out to

touch their coats as they passed, but they kept making notes
to themselves on their pocket organizers. *You have no pockets,*

I told them, but I might as well have been another dog for all
they listened. At the ocean, I threw stones. They skipped until

they sank and their sinking saddened me. What a sap! Every-
where, good looks and condescension: on the path above the

harbour my grade-six teacher, doubled over and gasping. *Enough,*
he ordered me. In the lava fields north of Terrace, the drunken

road boss asked my name again. I was walking and the fences
flew by so I could see right through them. I saw baseball teams

warming up for the big game. I saw children bent over fires of
their own making. I was walking and every step was a song. *Zooo*

Zah, Zooo Zah. Don't it make you want to cry. My feet flung
themselves out in front of me. They had a mind of their own.

They were bags of sugar, way ahead of me. There was no telling
how far I had come. Houses passed like frames in a movie. One

minute there was a river, the next a mountain. On a patch of alpine
snow, I paused to take in the view: ships in the strait heading for

Japan, fishermen letting the small ones go. I could hear a sea lion
barking. Pretty soon I was in Dublin. Round and round St. Stephen's

Green. Up and down the sniffy Liffey. Some kid on a Honda popped
a wheelie and held it. Nobody breathed. When his front tire touched

the road again, decades had passed, and my pockets were full of
flyers. They were bulging with *Watchtowers* and *Awakes*. I could

get a free beer at any bar in Mexico. The trouble was I was losing
too many friends. All this walking was taking me nowhere and the

Christmas decorations were starting to hurt my eyes. I was walking
through businesses on the esplanade. I was walking into market trends

and dollar cost-averaging. The landscape was all condominiums and
time shares and Queen Anne eclectic. Somewhere around the turn

of the century I stumbled upon the house I'd grown up in. Apples hung
on the tree in the backyard like planets on the verge of extinction.

Someone in my ex-bedroom waved at me and I waved back. I sat in
the old kitchen again, the toaster full of raisin bread and a pot of tea

on the table. I told the girl at the sink I'd been on a bit of a ramble.
I thought maybe this girl was my sister the way she kept nodding her

head. I thought she might even be my wife. The back door was open,
and the morning sun poured in across the tiles of red linoleum. I took

my tea out onto the porch and leaned into the railing. Sooner or later
her name would come to me.

Demobilization: The First Fifty Years

Once the world
was much worse than it is now.

Everybody promised
they'd never let it get so bad again,
like lovers who'd taken their craving
a little too far.

Women told men
they deserved a long rest.
Men told women they were glad
it was over. *To be home*, they sighed,
just to be home.

They made movies about themselves
and invited all their friends to watch them.
Years later they watched the movies again.

Remember those hats?
That song?

People behaved well.
They adjusted rabbit ears and
put their empty bottles
where the milkman could find them.

For a long time
they managed to keep themselves
busy: another reunion,
another funeral.

Some days they'd stop to talk
about their houses, the tree-lined streets,
the lilac coming into bloom.

Look! they'd say.
Look what we've done!

One for the History Books

The lizard stalks a fly,
a stalk himself until he moves.
Then, the bougainvillea becomes
bougainvillea with lizard.

The chaise longue looks to the sea,
soaks up sun in our absence.
When we lie down,
we disappear.

Last night, the rains came.
At first we thought flies were stinging us.
We hopped on the big red tiles
waving our arms, dripping.

You refused to open your mouth to the sky.

The policemen's barbecue broke up early
to our relief. Who would we phone
to complain about the noise?
We could see their green uniforms,
hear their laughter. One of them stirred something
in a large clay pot.
It was really quite touching.

I tell you I want a picture
looking out our hotel window, its panes
set in wrought iron,
those heavy blue curtains.

"This is our house," you tell me. "We live here."

I get the camera anyway.
This is something I'd like to hang on to.

Heathcliff Reflects on the Solstice and Marriage

Winter's back, as ugly as the woman I sleep with.
Another four months pulling myself around
in the dark, guessing at scars that brush
my lips. The season of trains,
of lines in general.

The season of clay.

Time enough to sweep out the workshop,
clean the gutters. Time enough
to buy our children out of slavery.

Worthy projects every one,
but what about love?

I hear you.

The sky is threatening. The grass
has given up. A class from the daycare
across the street troops by, snacks in hand.
I've never felt more like murder in my life, some
of those kids are that good looking.

Why, after all the jibes, all the
taunts and low remarks, she still wants to
keep me on, I'll never know.

Give me your paw is all she says, her lazy
eye pulling me down, the purple
birthmark across her forehead a
second smile.

And I do, claws itching, maybe a
whole December minute moving through
us while she guides me in as close
as rain, her throat exposed,
just begging for it.

California Was My Sister

I found her
beside a tidal pool above the beach.
Even in winter
I would lie with her and look
at the anemones, the sleek bullheads.

We talked about the sun,
about cars with roofs that rolled down.

I brought her home,
told everyone California was my sister.

In a week she was blonde and wearing make-up.
She bought magazines with pictures of Natalie Wood.

When she opened the door to her yellow room,
she crossed the borders of my parents' patience.

Talk spread:
Where have the old flags gone?
Somebody has been putting coins in the fountain again!

In my sleep,
the slamming of bedroom doors
and my father's words breaking like waves.

Before I knew it, California had gone,
the way Christmas goes, inevitably,
nothing but sorrow in its wake.

But sometimes when the weather is warm,
I still go down to the bay
and pronounce the names I have learned:
Santa Barbara, Fresno, Los Angeles.

I imagine a desert, palm trees,
streams of water.
I lean close to the surface of the sea
and remember Friday evenings in the front hall,
a door opening onto our dark veranda,
my sister's hair a torch,
lighting up the night.

The Origins of Money

Sand dollars, fragments of shells and
bottle caps — Coke, Orange Crush,
Fanta — in paper bags under my bed.
Hot summer nights, the air of my room dense
with crab, seaweed and low tide.

Sometimes the husks of chestnuts I have
picked from the boulevard, big as
golf balls, dark brown like the Mason and
Risch upright that has never moved
from its place in the living room.

Dreams where everything valuable appears
at my feet: Popsicle sticks, certain rocks,
a fifty-cent piece.

On lucky days, a discarded bottle that brings
two cents at the corner store, two pennies
I give back for gum, jawbreakers, a stick of licorice,

or take home, drop one by one through
the slit in the back of Koko, the hollow
brass monkey on my bureau.

The pay stubs my father stacks in a shoebox,
the pass book he hands to a teller.
The cards he slips into a gray wall clock,
his arm shuddering as a deep internal piston
impresses minute and hour.
Envelopes full of cancelled cheques
made out to people he cannot remember
for things he no longer owns.

Currency, current, what flows
between people and disappears. The dead
skin they shed, bits of themselves
that pass unnoticed.

The weight of it, the slow accumulation
of copper and silver inside Koko's thin walls.
The key that unlocks him, the contents
I pour across the bedspread
of my bed like a doomed villain just before
the temple walls collapse, eyes rolling
at treasure chests of gold, arms buried in jewels
right up to the shoulder.

The Birth of Tragedy

Pierre told his mother he was lonely.

"Loneliness is the human condition," she said. "Look at Spinoza."

"Spinoza was a nerd," Pierre said.

"Go to the park," she said, "if you're going to be that way about it."

So, off Pierre went. The park was knee-deep in squirrels. They'd chewed the tire swing into Swiss cheese again, and the slide was sticky with their urine.

A woman with a bum leg was making the rounds, fishing for empties in the trash bins.

"You got any kids?" Pierre asked her.

"I'm glad you brought that up," the woman said. "People don't take much interest in family these days."

"I'm looking for someone to play with," Pierre said.

"Help me sort through this garbage first," she said, tipping a can on its side.

Pierre knelt beside her, and together they separated candy wrappers, condoms, plastic bags full of dog shit from Coke cans and other returnables.

"So?" Pierre said after a few minutes.

"You're too late, I'm afraid," the woman said. "I sold both of my boys last Tuesday."

"You must be an awful mother," Pierre said.

"Or a liar," she said. "What would William of Occam say?"

"Non sunt multiplicanda entia praeter necessititatem," Pierre said.

"That's terrible Latin," the woman said. "No wonder you have no friends."

"No," Pierre said. "I have no friends because I'm a logical positivist. My mind is so rooted in empiricism that I'm incapable of flights of imagination. People shun me because I'm boring."

"Poor boy," the woman said.

Pierre left her to her scavenging and walked over to the duck pond. A blind man sat on a bench, throwing crusts into the water.

"How do you know the ducks are eating your crusts?" Pierre asked him.

"I don't need to know," the man said. "I am satisfied simply to believe they are eating them."

"Is it enough to imagine these ducks?" Pierre asked. "Do you not wish to see them, too?"

"I do not have to behold the ducks in order to believe in them," the man said. "In fact, I believe in the ducks in order that I might behold them. What's more, unless I believe, I will not behold."

"I wish I might behold a friend I could play with," Pierre said.

"Ahh," said the man. "You are lonely. The French have done this to you. They have robbed you of your connection to the world. You can no longer trust the words of others and must live in the echo of your own thoughts forever. I pity you."

Those bastards, Pierre thought, and went home to plan his revenge.

Some Questions

Would I invent time
if I hadn't already been told
about it? Would I think of it
trailing behind me
like Ariadne's thread?
        A way out or in?

Do dreams about my father
mean anything at all?
        Seated always,
compelled into a chair at the kitchen table,
slave to the chemistry of
my brain, angry,
bitter to be summoned and
        from where?

Is it helpful to imagine
myself a certain type
        of person?
Do I trust the mechanic
because I am trusting,
        laugh because I am
good-natured? Can anyone tell me
        how I stop doing this?

When did a door closing
        become a metaphor?
Doors to bedrooms, in particular.
        The idea of thresholds
and sex.

Why isn't everyone
        afraid of heights?
        Why does falling mean less to some
and more to others?

Can dogs tell
when they are dreaming?
        Starving, do they dream of food? Lame,
of speed and high
jubilant leaps? And what of their waking,
their eyes opening onto the dust of
another hot afternoon?

Sentimental Education

> *"A young man about eighteen,*
> *with long hair, an album under his arm,*
> *stood motionless near the helm."* — Flaubert

At first I thought my life
wasn't memorable, so I didn't
        write about it.

When I returned from Europe,
my sister took me aside.
"The votes are in," she said.
        "You're a jerk."

I regretted putting my fist
through the windshield of my girlfriend's
car,
        but later I didn't.

The first time a friend
picked me out of a crowd,
I went home to examine my face
        in a mirror.
"What's there to recognize?" I wondered.

When it became clear my life
wasn't memorable, I began to write
        about it.

One day I told my young wife to fuck off,
        and she did.

A holy man spoke to me for a whole afternoon.
"You don't care," the holy man finally said.
        "The truth isn't important to you."

I came to believe
        these words defined me.

My father died, and then a few friends.
At their funerals, I couldn't say what I was feeling.
        Years later, I still can't.

Subverting the Young

A tribe in South America
gets rid of children
by turning the boys into men at twelve
in a ceremony where the older guys
gather with the younger
in a hut
and smear themselves with ashes
chant and tell stories until
at the end of two weeks
they all come out and presto

the boys are men
with all the responsibilities of men
such as staying out of the sun and
getting married and raising a family
which takes care of the girls' childhood too
thus ridding the community of
indolent youths who spend their time
in unproductive and protracted periods of
play during which nothing gets done and
many valuable resources are consumed.

My own son
spends hours in his room with his headphones
or out on his skateboard with friends
who like to grind their expensive toys
on the cement steps of public buildings
so this morning I put in a half hour with him
fogging up the bathroom while I shave
and he fixes his hair which is not really
the same as two weeks in a hut

but close
and when I detect a lull in our ablutions
him with his gel and me with my Barbasol
I say *What about it?*

Enough's enough.
Time to quit dragging your ass
after which he nods or twitches
and leaves me staring in the mirror
proud of myself and my solution
to the growing food bills and the constant noise

my only problem now what to do
with the extra space after the basketball hoop comes down
not to mention that eyesore
of a tree fort
which I will definitely bring up with my son
who is hopefully at this very moment
down at the bottom of the back steps
shoeless and shirtless
only a thin pair of boxers between him and
the damp February air
dropping his collection of CDs
logo-ridden T-shirts and cargo pants
one by one into the trash
my wife smiling down at the little guy
the way he's shivering in the cold
like a real trouper
which is what I'll call him when he comes in
maybe pour us both some coffee
black and strong.

Do It Yourself

The sundeck we installed only six months
        ago collapsed last night, crushing the neighbour's

fence, and today when I phoned the contractor
        to come and repair his work, he told me the fault

was my own for having chosen him, for not
        researching the marketplace and for neglecting my

responsibilities as a consumer, so, no, he would
        not come, and he would advise his fellow tradesmen

to have nothing to do with me or my wife
        whose judgment had given their business a bad name

and he was considering legal action for
        what his accountant had deemed lost income, a sum

of six figures, which I had better not try to
        stiff him on because he had the law on his side

not to mention a few friends in high places
        who would soon be receiving their own copy

of this very phone call, which he was taping
        as we spoke, just to be sure there were no misunder-

standings, no unresolved areas of dispute that
        I would bring up later as part of an ongoing campaign

of abuse I had insisted on engaging in against him,
        against the mother of his children, and, yes, against

them, too, the apples of his eye, who were suffering,
        goddammit, if such a pussy-whipped word like suffering

even came close to the horror of their lives these days
        at school, at the local park, at the music lessons he didn't

have the money to pay for, thanks to me and my
        tight-assed complaints about the quality of life, the endless

spiral of inflation and my blessed needs.

Arts and Crafts

Friends are a blessing,
but too many can be a burden.
They lead to a cluttered life
in which little of significance
is accomplished.
Winnowing can be useful
and fun. A good
compost is essential,
where former friends provide
nutrients for the next crop.

Friends make excellent place mats
and runners for long trestle tables.
At picnics, be careful not to
keep them in the sun too long
as they will fade.
Wash in warm water. Never use bleach.
They look their best when allowed to dry
over the back of a chair.

There's nothing better
than a friend or two on the back porch
just as the sun sets.
Rolled loosely and flavoured with port
the taste is evocative of another
time, when sailing ships plied
the seas, bringing home new
friends from continents
far away.

In the language of friendship
adjectives carry greater weight than verbs, and
idiom is as dense as Turkish bread.
All conversation is carried on
in the subjunctive.

Claim a tax credit
when the acquisition of a friend
is for the purposes of business.
You may enter a capital
cost allowance on schedule six,
a sum subject to thirty-percent depreciation
each year. The government
frowns on such deductions, but until
they change the law,
there is nothing they can do.

Hostages

We are the carcasses of insects, dry husks beneath the
spider's web. We are bits of broken shell that roll

in and out with the tide. We are the coins people dig out
of the ground, then bury again in their top drawers.

We are animals who eat vitamins when our owners'
backs are turned. We are birds flying in through open

windows only to leave again, our beaks full. Because of us
light spreads to the far corners of the earth. Because of us

the lakes reflect the sky back upon itself. Because of us
the details of human commerce grow more complex.

We are children, anxious to pull out our own teeth. We
are adulterers in city parks who force others from the path

in our self-absorption. We are civil servants, survivors
of the Second World War. We wake up in the hour before

dawn as we have done every day for fifty years. We have
never been to an institute of higher learning, and the moon

between office buildings has never looked bigger. As makers
of prosthetic limbs, we reconsider the human form. In some

places we are lizards walking the streets. We are waiting
for a change in the weather, some excuse to move on to the

next thing. At the market we haggle over the price of tomatoes.
We test drive brand new automobiles and order books through

our computers. Charities come to our houses. We give
them sacks of old clothes and promise more next week.

Under our sidewalks, the earth continues to heave. We stuff
shopping lists into our jacket pockets. They are the only diary

that accurately reflects our lives. If there were a mirror in
which we could see ourselves, it would show a portrait of

a family, vacation over, bags and suitcases already unpacked.

Brave

1950 Morris Oxford

I'm driving our first car again, Greenmantle,
the road no more than a cow path,
Ireland maybe or rural Maine.
The sky is open, the grass in the ditch thick and long,
one of those days Keats wrote about:
"the coming musk-rose, full of dewy wine."

Each gear is smooth, no double clutching, and
there are four: *four on the tree* we used to say. And, yes,
I always saw a tree.

Greenmantle was a false prophet,
at least he was in the novel, a book about
sacrifice and deceit, the best and worst.

We used a hand crank on cold days.
There were little yellow wings
for signals, even a blind on the rear window.
The woman selling it was near eighty
and just married. I remember her husband
winked at me as he took the cheque.

Sometimes you'd slide across the bench seat
and take the wheel, and I'd play my recorder to show you
I wasn't nervous. When reverse failed,
we took it as a sign.

In the rear-view mirror, someone wants to pass.

I pull off into a field ringed by bushes,
pistons rising and falling like soldiers
on parade,
and I'm thinking how much I love this car,
its many gauges: oil pressure, voltage,
the speedometer so much like
our bedside clock.

My Young Wife Once Confessed

My young wife once confessed
she thought of my hands as hers,

not possessively, as part of the
property she was entitled to upon

marriage, but as extensions of
herself, other limbs that could

shingle a roof, fashion a child's
bedroom out of a porch, useful

tools to augment her own powers
and lend her greater vision. Years

later, just today in fact, she said
the same thing about my hands,

about the railing I had just finished,
though this time I did not bring up

Romeo, how he wanted to be a
glove for Juliet to wear, a second

skin she might quicken, or failing
that, a bird on a string to come

when she tugged, both weak
images I used to think, especially

during our dramatic years, less so
now, a little hurt instead my wife

never mentions my legs, which
to me are even more impressive,

but in her eyes, not so much.

Picking Up the Kids

I

In the cramped foyer of
the now-closed Greek restaurant,
my daughter is sharing a beer
with the cook.

It's almost midnight. Someone
has turned off the restaurant's fountain,
and the white cloth vanes of the signature
windmill hang limp in the still air
as though the owners are declaring defeat
over and over again.

I have come a little early,
unable to settle into anything
like a book or the late, late national news.
I am jittery, a man looking
for something to do.

From where I stand in the shadows,
it's easy to see her black skirt, the white
blouse she ironed earlier, their two
bottles rising and tilting, even the single
cigarette they share.

The night is quiet, but all around me
the minions of spring are myopic with purpose,
dusting off their leather jackets, kick-starting
Nortons and Triumphs and
Vincent Black Lightnings. I can hear
cellophane packages of Sex Wax bursting open,
and the sound of surfboards
slipping into the season's first wave. I can taste lilac and
Nicaraguan rum and pine forests still covered
with snow. To breathe this air is to believe
I will live forever.

A light goes out in the restaurant, the front
door opens. My daughter is saying something
about the sea, how even this far away
she can still smell it.

II

Strawberry season, no sugar
in the house,
        and you,
ready to burst,
like the fruit that sits in a bowl
on our kitchen counter.

I tell you I remember
the evening we started this boy,
a cold October Friday, the wood stove
crammed with windfall, and
        the house tropical.
A Friday because there
was gin and our daughter was sleeping over
somewhere.

You wanted more wood on
the fire, told me to make it hot as Barbados.
        So we don't need our clothes, you said.

When I think of us that night,
it's always from above, as though
I'm a hidden camera, the living room
furniture laid out below
        like the set of a play.
Lamp in one corner,
the couch against a wall, the easy
        chair that rocked.

What did we think we were doing?
Did we think at all?

It's a mile walk
to the store. Fresh jam
for breakfast, we are thinking.
Doughy white bread.

   At the hospital, I leave
the car lights on. When the sun
rises in the maternity's third-floor window,
our son slips out asleep.

   III

Prospero humiliates Ferdinand,
tells Miranda
   he's a spy,
unfit to seek her hand. He makes them
work for their love.

I pull into the boyfriend's driveway and
honk twice. The curtains pull back
   and fall shut again.
A minute later my daughter slides into
the passenger seat, overnight bag in hand,
twisting the rear-view
   to see herself.

I remember you had to lie,
told your parents you were staying
   at a friend's,
while I waited around the corner
in my car.

She would do this forever, our daughter,
carve a rut between his place
   and home.
At night, you speak
into the dark bedroom ceiling above our heads.

We have to make it harder for her, you say.

My daughter's first apartment's
up a flight of stairs, its floors so twisted
        the windows don't close.
She painted the bedroom dark green,
and when I buzz her number
        she lets me in.

IV

The car radio is all about Yugoslavia,
how the country is slowly
        falling apart,
one of those items I'm not even aware
I'm listening to. The light is red, and
        the wipers come on intermittently.

In his white gi, my son might be
an apprentice butcher.
        Earlier, at the dojo
I watched him punch the air and kick,
each move uncertain, as though
        he were struggling
with a large cumbersome thought.

The light turns green and
we drive a block or two. This
is a night
        that is passing quietly
and I am content to let it go
without pushing for answers, his impressions
of the day.

They must have used bad bricks, he says,
meaning the country, Yugoslavia,
        the cause of its ruin
a matter of poor construction materials,
        inferior clay.

The commentator's words:
Falling apart, he'd said.
        In my son's mind
a tower of blocks, each state a creation
out of Lego or Tinker Toys.

He's right, of course,

about nation building, how it requires
a skilled hand,
        the right combination
of foresight and human will.

I like to watch the students spar.
Before he fights, my son bows
        to his opponent.

Too Long in the Sun

A surfboard stands at attention
outside the front door: green fibreglass,
dimpled wax, gritty with sand.

You pat its keel, a blessing of sorts,
thanks, at least, our son has made it
home again.

No vacant chair at dinner tonight,
no bed minus its sleeper.
The math of parents who can't stop
calculating.

But in the mirror, we are the ones
less substantial,
like photographs left a long time
in the sun. Our bones are
shrinking, we grow
smaller.

Dread multiplies,
ugly as the family silver
we pray will be stolen from us.
Still we pass it on, and lift our eyes
to the glittering foam of
the approaching beach.

Once the sight of you
blocked out my entire future.

Now what's coming
dwarfs us both. How I love
your sweet, insignificant
silhouette!

The Best Yet

We were going to Disneyland
on a train, the four of us,
the way families are supposed to,
except our daughter was past caring
and our son was kidding
himself.

It wasn't really Disneyland,
only Euro Disney,
and there'd been nothing but rain in Paris
for weeks.

The suburbs outside our window
were no prettier for being
French — less in fact.
What had we been expecting?
Not abandoned cars, not stunted fig
trees. Where were the lovers kissing?
Where were the old men on bicycles?

When the metro dropped us at the station,
we left the rail car like inchworms
who had reached the end
of a long branch.

Everything's free after you pay,
the clerk explained at the ticket booth.
Instantly, I felt younger.

We filled our empty cameras with empty film.
You said your picture ID might be
the best yet. Impossibly,
we walked into
Main Street, U.S.A.

Our daughter assured us
they were all identical: Disneyworld,
Disneyland.
Like Safeways, she said.

We lined up for the Mountain of
Doom. We lined up for the Temple of
Peril. We ate baked potatoes drenched in
Cheez Whiz. We bought pictures of
ourselves screaming.

And when the sun came out unexpectedly,
briefly, the effect was
not magical. There was
no awe.

Awe, our children told us,
would come later.

On the Juan de Fuca Trail, Sometime in Late Spring

There is no answer when I call my son,
nothing to break the relentless surf
that rises like a wall of white noise,
inescapable as gravity, the soundtrack
of every west coast hiker's dream.

No answer at all, just three rings
and my own voice telling me to leave a message.
I press the portable against my ear,
listen for a sound: something miraculous,
a boy at home on a Saturday afternoon.

People pass on the trail. They thread by,
look away from me, another yuppie with a toy phone,
even here, perched above these breakers,
among ferns and giant spruce,
man-eating salal.

My son is all distance now,
all hands off and sleeping late, coming in at three
from a rave,
not a good word to say about anything,
not a word at all,
like someone sworn to secrecy,
silent eater, wraith that lives among us,
who closes doors behind him so quickly
you'd think a demon was biting his heels.

A real parent would have forced him
to come on this walk,
as I used to force him when he was small,
when he had no choice: shoes, coat,

Let's go, sport.

The kind of parent
who draws a line in the sand
then dares his child to cross it.

False Impressions

The seat belts on the plane
sound like my father's
cigarette lighter,
        its muffled conclusion
of sprung
steel.
In this turbulent air
I am happy to think of wicks
drenched in solvent, flints and their
        pinwheel of sparks,
that first wave of burning
tobacco.

Out the window, a thunderstorm
gathers in the distance.
        Bolts of lightning
strike the ground below, animating
the clouds around us, as if
every few minutes
someone is taking our picture.

This time we have said
we are East Indian. On the way down
we were vegans. My wife
accepts her chick pea curry,
        dahl and nan
from the outstretched arms of a
flight attendant who reads
her passenger roster twice before
        letting go.

Our son is ill,
feverish with some foreign bug.
        He declines food,

and leans his forehead into his open palm
as though he is making an offering
of himself. These days
I feel less like a father and
more like someone who
has recommended what turns out to be
        a very boring film.

I fill out his customs declaration
for him, forgetting
        the machete he bought,
wrapped up tight
in the cargo hold, slicing its way
        toward Canada.
Later I will agree with the
customs agent that
under the light of the scanner
        it doesn't look harmless
at all.

Calavera

Cervesa-tired,
we run the gauntlet:

families on blankets,
bracelets, necklaces, fans,
painted fish.
A man's hammocks, another's
wooden spoons.
The boy who writes names
on a grain of rice.

No, gracias, no, gracias.

At the pottery spread
on the paving stones,
a final test:
Charon wanting his penny
before we leave the living,
cross over into sleep.

Barro negro, black mud of Oaxaca,
colour of plague.

A woman, child-size,
dress a shroud,
skin dark as the pots at her feet,
bubbles numbers into
the thick air.

Cups and bowls
no Mexican would consider,
my father's impatience boiling in me
like the malaria that dropped him flat,
while on all fours, she tells you
how much for this plate, for
those three jugs.

Later in the taxi
among balls of newspaper,
a gift.
You take the skull in your hands,
its ebony face a fist, its grin
vacant.

Do I say we lived a long life,
that water never tasted bitter again?
Should I tell you animals parted before us,
that others sat on their haunches as we passed?
Do I speak of success in real estate,
trees that bore fruit after a dozen
barren years?

It was miracle enough
we fell into bed together
one more time,
that in the morning we woke
to greet our son,
himself a kind of spirit,
the skull now on his desk
like the portrait
of a friend who has passed away,
placed there out of respect,
or superstition, or what lies
between.

Private Auction

My mother outside the side door
clutches her walker, leans on it
the way she must have imagined herself
leaning one day,
tennis-shot knees catching up with her,
the joints collapsing, taking her
earthward.

The taxi she came in rolls out of sight,
as though she told the driver to disappear
before we could call him back,
cut short her visit,
this unannounced arrival, her face
through the glass all business, tense
with purpose.

The movers showed up so early, she says,
she had no time to think,
to fuss which vase, which dress,
which paintings she'd like to take with her
from her apartment, this ground-floor
flat.

We roll her to a chair, for an hour
parade items like auctioneers:
brass cigarette box, ivory-
handled fish knives, mortar and
pestle.

Do I hear fifty? Do I hear seventy-five?
Sold to the lady in the front row.

When I was eighteen
my mother thrust a pair of boxes
in my hands, told me to
take what I wanted or she'd throw it all away.
I remember the sun
through my window, the blue walls,
motes of dust that hung
in the light.
We make some tea, talk about
the new place, only two rooms now.
Meals included, a hairdresser
on the premises. Happy hour every
Friday. When she says she's tired
I drive her back.

What she takes away comes
back to us again,
wrapped in blue tissue paper,
a bow on top, as birthday presents,
Valentine's gifts,
a gradual release into the world, controlled,
the disposition of goods
equitable, spread out among her children and
grandchildren like a layer
in an archeological dig, those artifacts
people leave behind, sometimes
willingly.

Remission

— for Larry

Find a canoe, one with some dignity,
a bit of history, but broken, in need of repair,
and stretch new canvas across its ribs,
pull the fabric to the gunwale tight and hold it
with a hundred copper nails so that
when you soak it under the bright summer sun
it will shrink even tighter, until a marble
dropped on its surface will bounce
almost as high again,

and once the cloth is sealed and
the miraculous copper keel attached,
paint the crescent hull in yellow so bright
that from a distance your friends will think
the moon itself has fallen on its back and
lies floating,

especially the friends you have invited
out onto the water today to practice saving each other
from an unexpected wave, a sudden shift
in weight, friends who do not want to get wet,
but do so because you have returned from
the weedy bottom of the lake itself,
throat full of silt, lungs awash,
to tell them how easy it is to go under,
even in the calmest weather,
families looking on,
the shore only yards away.

What We Wake Up To

It's late
when we decide to stop
drinking,
after midnight, the wind
scattering newspapers and
last year's leaves across our front lawn.
A tough time to
let go of anything: love,
liquor.

Once it was all hugs and
kisses,
like the sound of a window giving way
under the weight of a shoulder.
The way we fell through it
and got up again.

We watched pianos go up in smoke,
tents collapse around us
in the dark. We watched people
of good conscience
conspire to make the situation worse.
We listened to our own breath
on the pillow until
we could stand the sound no longer,
rising from our beds
to drink again.

Paralytic, we carried the days
upon our backs and
pushed our failing marriages
from weekend to
weekend. We nursed our
betrayals, sipped at them slowly
and spat them into the ears
of anyone who would listen.
Our indiscretions rolled out behind us
like the centre line of
a boring highway and we told ourselves
it was worth it.

Face down in the sorry flower bed
of a rental house we
no longer remember renting,
on our knees in the snow, flashlight
shining into our eyes:
we did what we had to
to get where we are.

What we wake up to
is the voice we love telling us
there's someone else. What we wake up to is
a bright room without heat, a river
full of stones. This is the landscape we
were born to. These are our
reluctant legs.

Dangerous Days

A pelican forgets how to fly.

He falls to the sea with no more grace
than a broken water pump.

Such a collision! I'm convinced
he must be in love.

Once you threw yourself away like that. Once?
What am I saying?

But when I threw you away,
there was no splash, not
even a ripple.

A day will come when we'll forget
all the phone calls, what it was like
to write those letters.

Everything will seem too brief.

But to fall like that! Who would
deny themselves?

Boats pass
full of passengers.
We shout and
wave, happy for the captain.

What a pleasure to leave our wet towels in the sun!

At first we were afraid of the waves, but now
we dive through them.

Perhaps you're tired of me. What of it?
I'm tired of me, too.

Brave

We were looking at the moon, a full one it seemed, though there
was some discussion about that, about which day precisely and for

how long, until it was decided it was okay to say the moon was
full as long as we knew we might be mistaken, a compromise

which satisfied everybody and allowed us to return to our quiet
lunar observations while a CD of Latin music played through the

outside speakers, each of the songs full, too, of swooping, senseless
lyrics that probably wouldn't have made us want to cry if we'd known

what they were saying, but we didn't, content, as we were with the
moon, to act on empirical facts alone — what looked full, what

sounded sad. The sea battered Mexico's volcanic coast like a
ruminant horned beast that refused to give up the fight. Across the

bay, a flag we originally thought the size of a soccer field hung in
the moonlit air, not fluttering as flags are said to do in a breeze, but

coiling and uncoiling the way a snake might if it were flattened out
to the thickness of silk and suspended from a pole. These three

things — the rising moon, the waves, the undulations of the flag —
didn't bring to mind anything so grand as Arnold's "ebb and flow

of human misery," but aligned seaward as we all were on our chaise
longues, like sentinels just settling into their watch, our legs extended,

backs upright, heads tilted to the sky, I couldn't help thinking — maybe
it was the Spanish refrain, I don't know, some hint of a hopeless cause

like love or war about to begin — that the four of us were courageous,
though not in the way heroes are said to be courageous, those people

who snatch small children from debris in the middle of swollen rivers,
but brave as my mother used the term on those occasions when another

pet sank beneath the soil of our back garden, or when on a morning
of rain and gloom I walked out the front door to school, lunch kit in

hand, the drawstrings of my hood pulled tight around my face, another
pointless day with the substitute teacher. "You're a brave boy," she'd

say, and I believed her, as I believed my family was brave simply for
sitting there on that tropical evening, like passengers on an ocean liner

who had left behind a country on the brink of ruin only to discover there
was no safe port left in the world, no haven that would take them in.

Moving Day

This morning
the wood cookstove
was burning hotter
than usual,
its firebox full of
seasoned oak,

and the air hung
so light and warm around us
that when the kitchen gave
a little lurch, then
righted itself,
we were not alarmed, hardly
surprised at all.

But when our old house
began to rise
like one of those glass elevators
my wife says
so perfectly recreate
her dreams,
we knew the day had taken
a different turn.

No wrenching nails,
no boards torn apart.
Out the front door,
nothing but space,
a long first step.

And after a few minutes,
we began to move
west
in the breeze, over
the lake, the
neighbour's barn.

A squirrel squatted
at the end of one roof beam, and
the mice woke to the
day, to the
curious sun that peered through
their secret holes.

For a while
we could glimpse
our home's footprint
from the bathroom,
then it was gone.

There was so much to say
that we said nothing,
convinced
as we had been that
the Age of Miracles
was over for us,

that our feet
had been planted on
this earth forever.

We marvelled in silence
at horizons
we had not imagined
spreading before us,

both my wife and I
gripping the window ledge,
our eyes tilted up
for a change.